SIC

Achieving Sustainable
Growth & Profitability

The Practical Application of
Strategic Innovation in Business

SIC - StrategicInnovation.Consulting

Published by **RELIANCE BOOKS COMPANY, LLC**

www.RelianceBooks.com
Email: Contact@RelianceBooks.com

ORDERING INFORMATION - **Quantity Sales:** Special discounts are available on quantity purchases by corporations, educational institutions, government units, associations, churches and some other qualifying groups. For details, contact the 'Special Sales' department or see our website.

Individual Sales: Reliance books publications are available at many bookstores as well as on Amazon.com. They can also be ordered directly from Reliance Books.

Printed in The United States of America.

Di Frances, John
Achieving sustainable growth & profitability: the practical application of strategic innovation in business / John Di Frances

p. cm.

ISBN-13: 978-0970990853 (paperback)

1. Innovation. 2. Strategy. 3. Strategic Planning. 4. Creativity in business. 5. Organizational change. 6. Leadership.

Editor: Sarah Webber

SIC - StrategicInnovation.Consulting

To all those who had a hand in making this book possible, both family and friends, for your steadfast encouragement and participation during the writing, editing and refining which followed. 'What is worth doing is worth doing well.'

SIC - Strategic Innovation. Consulting

SIC

Strategic Innovation Consulting

Other Books by John Di Frances

Minding The Giraffes: The People Side of Innovation (2012)

Reclaiming The Ethical High Ground: Developing Organizations of Character (2002)

JackBilt^{TM} A Company: Of Happy, Successful People (2001)

REAL STRATEGIC PLANNING: A CEO's Guide – Release 2016

Radical Leadership – Release 2017

Healthcare Leadership Rx – Release 2017

Please note:

To obtain the greatest benefit from this book, space is provided beginning on page 69 for taking notes as you read.

CONTENTS

Introduction

Giraffes are truly the primary agents of innovation.

Why the Giraffe?

You may be asking yourself, why is there a giraffe on the cover of this book? And what do giraffes have to do with achieving future sustainability? **Everything!**

In 2012, John wrote a book entitled, *Minding the Giraffes* in which he dubbed innovators "Giraffes" because of certain shared characteristics with their human counterparts. For instance, in the wild, giraffes are not only the tallest of animals, but possess extraordinary eyesight. Similarly, in a business environment, Giraffe Innovators are the visionaries.

These imaginative individuals play a vital role in the C-Level executive's never-ending quest for growth and sustainability. They are creative problem solvers, relentlessly driven to achieve strategic innovation.

Giraffes are long range thinkers, possessing the unique ability of 'seeing' and foreseeing not only strategic opportunities and solutions, but also the roadmap to implementation.

As this book defines the practice of Strategic Innovation in business, the "Giraffe" once again comes into our focus.

The Road Ahead

"You can't do today's job with yesterday's methods and be in business tomorrow."

- George W. Bush

Where We Are and What's Coming

As a C-Level Executive, what is your ultimate goal? You may have several, such as providing excellent products and services, outstanding customer service, a great workplace, a reputation as the market leader…

However, it is *undeniable* that these must all contribute to one overarching goal, without which the organization will not survive in the long term: **Achieving sustainable growth and profitability!**

All of your other goals have merit, but without sustainable growth and profitability, the ability to achieve those goals will be short-lived. Most companies are currently growing and are to some extent profitable or else (in this economy) they would have already gone out of business.

But is their growth and profitability sustainable over the long term? That is the crucial question. Today, some major corporations are 'playing games' to make their results appear sustainable. For instance, IBM, a company that for decades has enjoyed the reputation of being a top Fortune 100 company currently enjoys Fortune's 24th spot. Although over the past five years its earnings per share have risen, a quick look under the hood shows a quite different and, for shareholders, alarming picture.

During this same five year period, sales revenue has dropped a whopping 18.2% and net income fallen 11%. And IBM's profitability would have decreased even more, but for severe cost slashing which has further weakened the company's future prospects. Then, how has IBM's earning per share continued to rise, you may ask?

The key to IBM's slight of hand is termed 'Financial Engineering.' What the company's CEO and Board have done is to orchestrate large buy backs of IBM's stock, in itself not a bad idea. However, since profits weren't available to fund this maneuver, the company has borrowed $10 billion, yes, that's billion dollars of new debt.

Sustainable? No! But in the short term it does paint a rosy earnings per share picture and many less than savvy investors look no further than to this single metric. In many public companies, the CEO doesn't stay around long enough to reap the harvest of such actions. And as most have golden parachutes, they depart unscathed, leaving the next CEO to deal with the mess.

But in privately held, middle market and smaller firms and even smaller publicly held companies, this sort of of shenanigans won't work, not even temporarily. Thus, REAL growth and profitability, sustainable beyond the short-term are essential to the ongoing health and ultimate survival of the company.

In the past, sustainable growth wasn't actually all that difficult a hill to climb. Certainly, the new business five year failure rate has for a long time scuttled a daunting 80% of new ventures. But for companies which survived those brutal early years and especially those that made it to the end of their first decade, the majority could anticipate the likelihood of a long and prosperous future.

However, today, we are experiencing a new and unprecedented dynamic. "Business life" (the marketplace and the way we do business) has changed. It is a far more perilous journey. And there are two main reasons.

First, it is because the world has fundamentally changed and will not be returning to the old status quo. America is no longer protected by two great oceans. Ever increasing global competition has forever ended our geographic isolation. Moreover, as cost of production in China continues to rise, new competition is emerging from Vietnam, Cambodia and other low wage economies. But it won't end there. African countries which enjoy reasonable political stability are about to come on stream as the newest and lowest international wage centers.

American businesses can no longer compete on price! Not today and not in the foreseeable future.

But there is a second and even more dangerous trend facing American businesses across all industries, not just manufacturers, but also those in the professional services and retail sectors that have traditionally enjoyed immunity from foreign competition. What is this new and pervasive danger?

Disruption! Disruption is either already occurring or will soon occur in virtually every industry and at an increasing pace. Still more dangerous is the fact that, more frequently than not, in most industries the source of the disruption is **external** to that industry.

Who disrupted the telephone, music and other industries? Apple! Was Apple a telephone or music company? Certainly not. The fact that most industries are disrupted suddenly by players from outside of their industry which is precisely what makes these disruptions so unexpected, sudden and dangerous.

As a C-level executive, you know your company and you know your industry and you feel safe in that knowledge. However, what most executive leaders neither expect nor realize is who, outside of their industry is, at this moment, preparing to launch a new technology or unconventional business model that will yank the rug right out from under their business. The worst part is that if you are like the vast majority of business executives, you won't even see it coming. It will be a surprise attack, which for your business, could rival the scale of Pearl Harbor on December 7th, 1941. However, unlike the U.S. Navy, you may not have the resources and time to recover.

Think it won't happen to your organization? Think your business is different and immune to disruption?

Think again! That's what one pervasive worldwide

industry thought. Their business model was global, in most places, protected by strict government licensing which provided them with a captive market and even strict price protection because the supply was tightly controlled and price regulated. Furthermore, their business model had been successful for over 150 years. What could be more secure than that?

I'm referring to the taxi business. Horse drawn and then motorized. Its origin can be traced to Paris in 1640. Few businesses in cities around the world became more ubiquitous than the "taxi cab." That is, until Uber and Lyft burst onto the scene to disrupt it and, in just a few years have nearly destroyed the "taxi cab" business model. Are there taxis still around today? Of course. But the question is for how long and how much more will their market-share shrink with each passing year?

Did the taxi companies see it coming? Of course not. After all, **they were protected!** And that protection which came directly from the local city government where each taxi company operated, created a false sense of security. When the local city government ensures protection and we have sway over our elected municipal officials, what could possibly go wrong?

Security is, however, a two-edged sword. It often causes us to close our eyes to that which should be obvious. In the case of taxi companies — service. More often than not, poor service. Dirty cabs, surly or at best unconcerned drivers, poor driving, rate gouging by taking unaware passengers 'the long, slow way' while the meter keeps running...

Were all taxi companies and drivers bad actors? Certainly not, but enough were that passengers worldwide neither liked nor enjoyed their service.

And then there was convenience. Have you ever tried hailing a cab on a busy city street during rush hour or late in the evening? Or how about in a driving rainstorm?

Add to that the fact that their service is expensive. This toxic mix opened the door to a very unlikely disruptor. All it takes for major business model threatening disruption to occur in any industry is enough dissatisfied people or even just a single, dissatisfied person who decides that there needs to be 'a better way.'

In NYC, those taxi cab medallions embedded in the hood of taxi vehicles were virtual gold. They could be bought and sold at six figure prices and banks were eager to provide loans with the medallion alone, not the taxi cab, as collateral.

Try obtaining a loan or selling a medallion today. Each week their value declines and there is no end in sight. And what is the asset base behind Uber and Lyft? No hard assets. Simply an idea whose time had come. Nothing more! **And with that asset base of just an idea**, these two companies have in only a few years risen from nonexistence to stratospheric double digit billion dollar valuations.

At the same time, Apple is trying to disrupt the disruptor. In May of 2016, Apple announced that it was investing $1 billion in the Chinese ride-sharing company Didi Chuxing, the largest app-powered car service in China, a market in which Uber is aggressively trying to gain traction. Why has Apple chosen this investment? The reason is fourfold:

First, to counter Uber and Lyft, allowing Apple to gain a foothold in what it sees as the emerging techno-transportation marketplace. Secondly, because Apple's leadership believes that this investment will ingratiate the company with the Chinese government and thereby, reduce the government's resistance to Apple's product sales in China. Third, because Apple is actively competing against Tesla, GM, Ford, Fiat-Chrysler, Google and others, in the race to develop the self-driving car. Lastly, because ride-sharing services are powered by smartphones such as Apple's iPhone.

Imagine a day when you not only use your smartphone to hail a ride, but are then driven to your destination without the presence of a driver in the vehicle. A day when you can order merchandise and a driverless car or truck picks it up from the seller(s) and delivers it to your home or office within an hour or two. Will that be to the curb or will a robot step out of the vehicle and bring it to your door? Whatever the future of smartphone ride-hailing, delivery services and driverless vehicles — cars, trucks and drones — looks like, Apple wants its piece of the pie.

However, only time will tell if this is a smart strategy.

Meanwhile, Apple's numerous missteps in recent years gives one cause for doubt, as it has become clear that the company is slipping in terms of vision and strategy execution.

Back to Uber, their website tells the story succinctly.

"On a snowy Paris evening in 2008, Travis Kalanick and Garrett Camp had trouble hailing a cab. So they came up with a simple idea—tap a button, get a ride.

What started as an app to request premium black cars in a few metropolitan areas is now changing the logistical fabric of cities around the world. Whether it's a ride, a sandwich, or a package, we use technology to give people what they want, when they want it."

And I might add, where they want it.

Did you think that Uber's goal was to become a next generation taxi company? Or maybe to replace taxis? Not at all. The latter is but one of their long-term corporate strategies. Notice the words, *"the logistical fabric."* And *"Whether it's a ride, a sandwich, or a package, we use technology to give people what they want, when they want it."*

The words *"logistical fabric"* and *"technology"* should be a dead giveaway that Uber has something far grander in mind than merely replacing taxis in cities around the world. And notice I said "replacing," not "competing with" taxis.

Uber Technologies Inc. is an American multinational

company. WOW! Talk about vision. Yes, they are definitely in the transportation business and their website states as much, using the word *'transportation.'* But the legal corporate name of the parent corporation doesn't even include the word 'transportation.' What it does include, other than the words "Uber" and "Inc." is "Technologies." What does that tell you about the strategic vision of Uber's leaders?

And far more importantly to you, when will a bright idea become the genesis of disruption within your industry? It's no longer a question of 'if,' only 'when.'

My purpose is not to frighten you, but to make you aware of the clear and present dangers facing your industry and business. Although what you see developing **within** your industry may present some level of danger, it is what you don't see, developing outside of your industry, that is a far greater threat.

So, how do you escape from the twin dangers of ever increasing global competition and internal as well as external market disruptors? There are two ways.

The first is to sell out now, pocket the money and retire to the Bahamas or a similar tax haven and spend your days lying on the beach. Appealing? Possibly, depending upon your company's worth and your life goals.

Realistically, your only other choice is to become the 'Disruptor' in your own industry. If you are the first to act, you can prevent others, both inside and outside of your industry, from doing it to you. That is the unique advantage of being the 'first-mover.'

Remember, all it takes is for one bright kid to see an opportunity to improve upon something you do or meet a need of your customers in a new and innovative way. And that customer need will most likely be something that you are not even aware of today. Most organizations discover their customers' needs by asking their customers. However, this is not the best method because it is based upon the premise that customers actually <u>know</u> what they want and need.

If you had conducted a survey on the streets of NYC ten years ago, how many people would have listed a smartphone based ride-hailing service, much less a car service that would efficiently and economically deliver purchases to their home or office within minutes of placing an order? What customer would have responded to retail stores' focus groups suggesting an Amazon.com? Or would an Apple customer focus group in the 1980s understand that what they really wanted was a GUI (Graphical User Interface) computer, minus a fan so that it would operate silently or featuring a mouse with only one button? Not likely!

As a general rule, **profoundly innovative ideas**, those destined to give your company a strategic advantage, do not result from discussions with customers, surveys or focus groups. If you assume that your customers are the best source of innovative ideas to give your company a competitive advantage in the marketplace, I'm afraid you will be disappointed. Your customers may be a source, which you neglect only at your own peril, but they do not come even close to being a wellspring for ground-breaking and innovative new ideas.

Or maybe you are thinking that it would be impossible for your company to become your industry's disruptor. You're just too small. No, the potential is there. In fact, you already possess most of what it takes. You have a market position, however large or small, knowledge, experience, people and other resources.

Size is not a limitation. Remember what Steve Jobs said in 1998 about the battle with Apple's behemoth competitor, IBM.

"Innovation has nothing to do with how many R&D dollars you have. When Apple came up with the Mac, IBM was spending at least 100 times more on R&D. **It's not about money. It's about the people you have, how you're led, and how much you get it."**

*But w*hy is it necessary to simultaneously pursue both well conceived strategies <u>and</u> breakthrough innovation? Isn't one such strategic advantage sufficient?" No, you definitely need both, because they are two sides of the same coin. Or, to look at it another way, strategy and innovation form a continuous loop.

You need innovative thinking to create your organization's key strategies and you need the right strategies to focus and drive innovation for maximum ROI. Innovation & Strategy operate synergistically to form a continuous and highly effective means of achieving sustainable growth and profitability.

What is your company missing which will produce sustainable growth and profitability? Just three things:

1. An organizational culture which is vibrant, motivated and excited to participate in viral open innovation which is strategically directed for maximum long term growth, profitability and ROI.

2. An effective strategic mindset, a pattern of thinking and vision as well as a full arsenal of aggressive strategies to drive the needed innovation.

3. And lastly, the commitment to **Just DO IT NOW!**

Remember the discussion a few pages back about Uber? Given their name, **Uber Technologies Inc.**, how big a role do you think **Innovation, Strategy** and **'Just DO IT NOW!'** plays in the minds of Uber's leaders?

The purpose of this short book is to demonstrate that strategy and breakthrough innovation are crucial to achieving sustainability and moving your company forward to becoming your marketplace's disruptor and ultimately, its leader.

A Case Study in
Strategic innovation

It's Easy to Miss the Forest
for the Trees

What often appear to be the most obvious and immediate solutions, frequently result in the creation of unforeseen and far larger long term problems.

Things Often Are Not What
They Appear to Be

For nearly one hundred years, the U.S. Forest Service sought to prevent forest fires using every conceivable means, including the famous icon, Smokey the Bear. At first, these efforts appeared to work as the number of forest fires caused by humans significantly declined while the number of visitors to national parks and forests increased annually. But was this appearance of success real. Did this strategy achieve the goal of protecting our national forests and parks?

Unfortunately not. Despite a decrease in the number of fires, to the dismay of the Forest Service, the intensity of fires increased. Why? The Forest Service's fire prevention measures had, over time, inadvertently created the necessary tinder for fueling large scale fires.

While periodically occurring fires burn off ground based, low hanging growth and rarely threaten the larger trees, they also serve to prevent the build-up of kindling that fuels the less frequent, but immensely devastating fires which destroy entire forests. Native Americans understood this and regularly started fires for the specific purpose of clearing brush.

Corporate culture can sometimes mimic the Forest Service's short term focused and most importantly, ultimately unsuccessful problem solving approach. Senior executives all too often focus on symptoms and target specific actions without a clear understanding of how those actions will impact the organization as a whole. As a result, we sometimes create more serious problems in the process of attempting to solve lesser ones. Remember the story from your childhood of the king who wanted to rid his palace of mice?

The U.S. Forest Service eventually conquered the problem by applying the ancient Native American practice of setting fires to cause prescribed burns. It worked like a dream, restoring ecological balance to the parks and forests.

In business, we must be wary of the most obvious and immediate solutions. With careful research and creative thinking, we can achieve integrated innovative solutions for optimal strategic outcomes without creating new and bigger problems.

Essential Practice #1: Changing Your Game

Innovation is not a simple process produced through a rote series of cookie-cutter steps.

Strategically Directed
Open Innovation

Innovation is the first requirement for sustainable growth and profitability, but what is meant by the term "innovation"? Is it merely the generation of an endless stream of new and creative ideas?

No. While idea generation, also known as 'Ideation,' is a critically important element to innovation, many CEO's say that they've tried innovation and although it resulted in an avalanche of new and often creative ideas, the ideas proved to be impractical and the organization was unable to successfully implement them to its advantage.

Ideas alone do not equal innovation. Then what is innovation and how can an organization best utilize this resource to consistently produce positive bottom line results?

Peter Drucker defined innovation as *"Change that creates a new dimension of performance."* I agree with him, but with two additional words: ***"Change that creates a new dimension of highly beneficial performance."*** I believe Drucker inferred the words 'highly beneficial' here, but I also believe that it is far too important to presume that all who attempt to engage in innovation will understand this caveat instinctively.

Not all ideas are beneficial to the organization. Ideas must result in a strategic advantage, be value driven and capable of implementation. In short, to be of any use at all, they must be "highly beneficial" in yielding an increased ROI.

This brief book provides a basic understanding of strategic innovation in business; for a more complete picture of what innovation is and is not, I recommend that you read my book, *Minding The Giraffes: The People Side of Innovation*. Here, it will suffice to review why innovation is no longer optional, but an absolute requirement for sustainability.

Let's begin by taking a deeper look at the key concepts of my definition for business innovation:

Change - Non-negotiable! It simply is what it is. Without real 'change,' there can be no innovation. Innovation is the opposite of the status quo. If you and your organization are wedded to the status quo, literally 'to the past,' you will not benefit from reading this book. You cannot hope to reverse a downward trend or fend off a disruptor without a major transformation. **Today, accelerating change is the constant in business.** Highly effective leaders not only embrace continuous change, they seek every way possible to employ it for their strategic advantage.

that creates - Something must be created for innovation to exist. Often, company executives are more willing to embrace incremental change. There is certainly nothing wrong with that, but if you think about it, incremental change does not actually <u>create</u> anything. And it does not satisfy the next criterion of innovation.

a new dimension - Here is the crux of what makes innovation so incredibly powerful in business. Real innovation is not incremental. It's breakthrough, leap-ahead change. Change that disrupts the status quo and that disruption can be internal to the organization as well as external, impacting the organization's industry and markets. The fact is that change resulting from innovation almost always begins internally, changing the leadership's mindset, the vision, paradigms and practices of the organization itself, thereby positioning the organization so that it is capable of taking rapid action to disrupt its markets and industry whenever an opportunity arises.

of highly beneficial - There must be a highly positive benefit. I've visited companies that spend an enormous amount of resources 'playing at innovation.' These activities do not produce any real benefit and result in no real innovation. Highly beneficial means the effort must produce a significant increase in ROI.

performance - This is where the rubber meets the road. It is the measure of the benefit. Performance benefits can be manifested in many forms, i.e., increased revenues, better products/services, new markets created or opened, improved organizational culture, morale and productivity, quantum leaps in quality, efficiency, service, reliability… In whatever dimensions it occurs, it must be real, tangible and measurable.

This is what business innovation demands and anything less is not true innovation. **If it does not incorporate all five of these criteria, it is not real innovation.**

But there is far more to the sphere of innovation — another powerful dimension which can result in the achievement of exponential outcomes.

Open Innovation

How is open innovation different? Traditional innovation occurs internally, utilizing the knowledge, experience and other resources available within your organization. Open innovation is simply that, opening the organization up to the very best of what the outside world (the world outside of your organization) has to offer.

In the past several decades, many companies pursued industry benchmarking as a competitive strategy. Whatever industry they were in, unless they were the undisputed industry leader, they sought to mimic whatever the leader did. Such "me too" tactics resulted in many companies becoming the 'Avis' of their industry, namely, #2 and proud of it.

Open innovation looks beyond whatever the industry leader or your competitors are doing. Alerting you to what other organizations, the best of the best, are thinking and doing all across the globe, in dealing with opportunities and issues similar to those you are facing.

Open innovation is simply expanding your horizon and opening your organization to fresh thinking and problem solving without regard to the status quo of your company, industry or country. Or do you really believe that your organization and industry have the best paradigms and "ways of thinking" regarding ideation, innovation, change, disruption and the future? Better than anyone else — anywhere in the world? Inconceivable? Sadly, I've been introduced to organizations where the senior executives firmly believed and even stated that this was the case.

However, the response I normally hear from executives is, *"Our business/industry is too unique to find outside solutions relevant and adaptable."* I have consulted for more than 30 years globally within the aerospace and defense industries, healthcare, technology, consumer products, financial, manufacturing, software, professional services and other industries — companies ranging from Fortune 100's to start-ups as well as nonprofits and government agencies.

While, I have found that real 'rocket science' truly does exist (particularly in the aerospace, defense and bio-medical industries and in basic research), overall, I've encountered very little that is real 'rocket science' or even truly unique. What I have found is people around the globe struggling with similar problems and opportunities in unique settings.

Same issues...different (unique) settings. And what I have consistently discovered is that the best solutions frequently had broad implications and application across many other organizations and industries.

As the famed King Solomon, observed three thousand years ago, *"There is nothing new under the sun."* By far, most of the uniqueness that clients have related to me about their businesses has been the outgrowth of their own perceptions. They saw everything about their business and industry as being totally unique; therefore, it was, at least in their minds.

But in reality, it wasn't! Not even remotely! However, when all of your knowledge and experience is tied to one field or industry...then everything appears to be unique. Or to put it another way, when you have been a carpenter all your life, every problem is a nail and requires a hammer to solve. And when that doesn't work, there is always a bigger hammer to be found.

Open innovation is an amazing cure to the myopia caused by operating within a closed box. Just as opening windows on the first warm day of spring clears and freshens the air inside, open innovation throws open the door to new ways of thinking and 'seeing' otherwise unimaginable.

With fresh thinking and a bolder vision which open innovation brings, all manner of internal and external breakthroughs suddenly become possible. How many true breakthroughs has your organization accomplished in the past year? The past six months? Were there any last month? Will there be any this month?

Without innovation, your organization is, at best, treading water. But you say that you are experiencing growth and profitability. That may well be true, today,[1] but the question is, 'What will happen to that growth and profit when your industry is disrupted?' And remember, it's not a question of if. Only when disruption will occur!

How can I be so certain? If taxi cabs didn't convince you, let's look at a few more examples.

At the end of 2010, Nokia enjoyed an amazing 31% of the mobile phone marketplace. They were without question the undisputed industry leader with 124 million phones shipped in just the 4th quarter of that year. In September 2013, Nokia announced that its phone and services business would be sold to Microsoft for $7.2 Billion. The acquisition closed in April 2014 and was hailed by Microsoft's then-CEO, Steve Ballmer, as *"…a bold step into the future — a win-win for employees, shareholders, and consumers of both companies."* In mid 2015, just over a year following the acquisition, Microsoft took a $7.6 billion dollar impairment charge, writing-off the Nokia acquisition. Nokia's phone business was DEAD!

Remember E. F. Hutton? What about MCI Worldcom, Border's Bookstores, Arthur Anderson, General Foods Corporation and DeLorean Motor Company or the multitude of airlines which have ceased to exist in recent years. Not convinced? How about Kodak, the 124 year old corporate giant that dominated the world of film and filed for bankruptcy protection in early 2012?

A study from Washington University's John M. Olin School of Business estimates that 40 percent of today's Fortune 500 companies whose stock is listed on the S&P 500 will no longer exist in 10 years. Still a skeptic? By the end of 2015, only 13% of the companies listed in the Fortune 500 in 1955, only sixty years earlier, still existed. And when we talk of Fortune 500, we are speaking of the largest companies in the U.S.A., not small or medium sized businesses.

However, I've saved the best for last. In 2015, in presenting his last annual speech before retiring, John Chambers, CISCO's visionary CEO, told the audience, *"Forty percent of businesses in this room, unfortunately, will not exist in a meaningful way in 10 years."* Ouch! That room was filled with executives from many of the best and brightest companies from around the world.

Chambers warned companies that they could not *"miss a market transition or a business model"* or *"underestimate your competitor of the future — not your competitor of the past"* if they want to survive. ***"Either we disrupt or we get disrupted! Startups want to upturn every existing business,"*** Chambers said.

Apart from open innovation, your business is also likely to meet an untimely end. Fortunately, this need not be the case. A thriving culture of on-going open innovation can result in your company becoming a driver, if not the leader in your industry. Strategic open innovation, is your first step in creating a sustainable, competitive advantage through the consistent achievement of internal as well as marketplace breakthroughs.

SIC - StrategicInnovation.Consulting

Essential Practice #2: Real Strategic Planning

If you haven't invested time into
serious strategic thinking,
you have no real strategies.

Strategic Planning Begins With Strategic Thinking

Recognizing the Problem

Executives frequently do not realize that **strategic thinking** is an essential precursor to strategic planning. Instead, they dive into what they believe will be an effective strategic planning exercise. In fact, they are often surprised to learn that just because their efforts have resulted in a formal plan, it is not a "given" that real strategic thinking has actually occurred.

Why then is this crucial phase of planning so often overlooked? Because a common misconception exists in regard to strategic planning. Aren't strategic thinking and strategic planning the same thing? No!

Like every organization, yours needs effective strategies to produce tangible results in terms of growth, profitability and sustainability. Thus, your goal is to develop a strategic plan to ensure the organization's future. At this point, you find yourself at a pivotal juncture where the imperative of strategic thinking must first be addressed. It is foundational and cannot be ignored without suffering consequences.

Is Your Strategic Plan Strategic?

The missing ingredient in the majority of Strategic Planning efforts is STRATEGY! When I speak to executive audiences on this vital issue, I begin by asking two questions. *"How many of you have a Strategic Plan?"* All of the hands go up. Then I ask the second question, *"How many of those plans contain numbers, budgets, spreadsheets?"* Once again, typically everyone's hand goes up. Then I say, *"You do not have a Strategic Plan. What you have is an Operating Plan."*

Most so-called 'strategic plans' are merely operating plans, together with a rehash of Vision and Mission Statements and dominated by reams of spreadsheets detailing sales projections and operating budgets. They represent 'tactical', not 'strategic' thinking.

What is the difference between the two? The strategic planning process first identifies possible and emerging marketplace opportunities as well as threats, a SWOT Analysis (Strengths, Weaknesses, Opportunities and Threats). This, some companies regularly include, but typically only in regard to existing, known opportunities and threats, with little or no consideration of those which are emerging outside of their industry. In addition, very few invest in the most critical next step, wherein the Leadership Team brainstorms, investigates, evaluates and selects those innovative ideas with the best potential for internal or marketplace disruption. Bringing various skill sets to the table, they then collaborate to develop a plan incorporating innovative new strategies for creating breakthrough growth and profitability.

Strategic business plans should be concise, specific, actionable, relevant and time-bounded, not a lengthy document that gathers dust on the shelf. Progress in implementing the plan should be continuously monitored and when circumstances change or new information is learned, the strategic plan quickly adjusted. **The greatest value of any strategic planning exercise is derived from what is discovered and learned in the process, through critical thinking, active investigation and constructive discussion among the organization's leadership.**

Strategic Planning should result in a high level 'strategic plan', identifying key issues and strategies, not operating numbers. The reams of spreadsheets belong in your operating plan, not the strategic plan. The actual strategic plan should in many cases be a series of one-to-five page creative strategies regarding open innovation of, products/services, marketing, sales, staffing, systems and other disruptive opportunities which result from the exercise of carefully thinking through the near, medium and long term future. From this, the organization can then create an operating plan with the financial projections needed for managing daily operations.

Today, many companies have adopted the viewpoint that as the medium term future — anything beyond three years — is so uncertain, there is no need to think strategically or plan beyond that point. In many industries, this makes sense in regard to the operating plan, but never in regard to the organization's strategic plan. In planning, short term is 1-2 years (the current timeframe), 3-5 years (medium term) and more than 5 years (long term). Obviously, the level of specificity and detail decreases as your plan moves outward, but a strategic plan that ends at three years is extremely shortsighted.

Strategies by their very nature have long term impacts, even if their implementation occurs over a more immediate timeframe. Think about the marketing disasters resulting from short term decisions, such as the introductions of New Coke, Betamax video, Bic Underwear, Harley Davidson Perfume, Coors Rocky Mountain Spring Water, Clairol's Touch of Yogurt Shampoo...and the list goes on and on. Major corporations with large, sophisticated marketing departments and huge advertising budgets creating major product blunders. Despite the uncertainties, not to think through your organization's future; its products/services and markets is like climbing a mountain wearing a visor that severely reduces your field of vision to the next hundred feet above you. How could you possibly select the best route to the summit when your vision is so limited?

In contrast to the strategic plan, the purpose of an operating plan is to efficiently quantify and assign resources within your organization in support of the strategic plan. Both are essential, but most companies plod through year after year with only an operating plan, yet assuming they have a strategic plan. Is it any wonder that few of those companies experience the sustained breakthrough, profitable growth their senior executives desire? Exceptional and even exponential results are the outcome when the operating plan is based upon a well conceived and considered strategic plan designed to propel the organization forward rapidly. Think of it this way: If Part B is the operational plan, then Part A is the Strategic Thinking and Planning which logically must precede the creation of Part B. You do not build a house by beginning with the first floor. Establishing a firm foundation is just as essential in strategic planning as in house construction.

The Solution

The challenge lies in how the organization's leadership team can create the optimal strategic plan. Only a process involving strategic thinking and the effective collaboration of your leadership team is capable of producing a winning synergistic outcome.

The heart of innovation is thinking. This requires a dedicated investment of time and energy. All members of the leadership's strategic planning team must be fully empowered and working together collaboratively in the development of innovative solutions and strategies through pooling collective knowledge and actively engaging in open dialogue and inquiry, while simultaneously abandoning restrictive preconceptions. This 'all-in collaborative engagement' creates the dynamic for successful strategy creation.

The final step is to develop your strategic action plan,

for without taking action, the planning process is pointless. Its goals and solutions must be practical, affordable, capable of implementation and measurable.

The Value of an Experienced, Professional Facilitator

A highly skilled, professional facilitator with extensive cross-industry business experience can accelerate the development of your organization's strategic plan by freeing your leadership team to focus solely on sharing ideas openly and thoroughly evaluating existing and emerging opportunities for a synergistic outcome while minimizing threats. The facilitator engages your team in an intensely collaborative exercise where problems and potentialities can be viewed from every possible perspective.

To the surprise of many, CEO's and COO's are not optimally positioned to lead the strategic planning effort. As a senior executive, you are highly skilled at leading staff meetings on a regular basis, however, routine staff meetings are typically directed at issues that are information and decision centered. These require knowledge and experience that is resident within the organization. By contrast, strategic thinking and planning, innovation, ideation and complex problem solving should draw heavily upon external ideas, resources and collaborative thinking (the essence of Open Innovation). Thus, a professional facilitator with broad rather than industry specific knowledge and experience can enrich and accelerate the process.

It is imperative that your organization has ready access to outside ideas, ways of 'seeing' and doing that bring with them the fresh breeze of strategic thinking and open innovation. Quite literally, for real change to occur, PARADIGMS MUST BE BROKEN! Whether or not you are aware of it, if you have been doing anything the same way for the past five years, you are most likely already operating at a competitive disadvantage today, such is the rate of change. And that rate is constantly accelerating!

Successful Application

Intent without action is as effective as a Ferrari without gasoline.

Now That You Know,
What Will You DO?

There is an old saying that "Knowledge is Power." This is true, but only if that knowledge can be effectively put to use effectively. Knowing what to do is of no use whatsoever, if you fail to act or procrastinate until it is too late.

"The early bird does indeed get the worm!" The dilemma facing your business and industry is that there is likely to be only one worm and thus, one company will get it. When it comes to market disruption, there rarely is a second place prize.

Think your business is too small to successfully become the disruptor? Likely not. In fact, if you are small, you probably have a very distinct advantage over your larger competitors.

If your company is large, it has the advantage of more resources. However, companies are like ships. My speed boat can turn on a dime. It's small and nimble. Granted an aircraft carrier has enormous fire power, but it takes a very long time to get underway and an even longer time to turn.

To become the disruptor you do need a little bit of firepower, but speed and agility are far more important. Innovation, especially strategic open innovation requires moving fast! Faster than your competitors.

When you fill the gas tank on your car or truck, it typically takes two or three minutes for 12-20 gallons. When an IndyCar race team pit crew does it, they fuel 18.5 gallons and change four tires as well as adjusting the front and rear wings and suspension, all in 8 seconds or less. To become a disruptor, your organization needs to begin thinking and acting like an IndyCar race team.

Will positioning your organization to become the disruptor of your marketplace be hard work? Yes! Is it fun? It certainly can be, if you make it fun and create an environment where people literally 'love to come to work to WIN!'

Is it doable? Yes, but only with your full commitment. And not just in word. You must lead from the front. That does not mean that you have to magically become the Chief Creative Innovator and Strategist of the organization. These may or may not be your natural gifts. What you must become is what I term the "CIA.' The Chief Innovation Advocate!

If you buy-in whole-heartedly and demonstrate it, supporting the Giraffe(s) within your organization, your people will too. If you only pay it lip service, so will your people. You are their leader. They will follow your lead, for better or worse.

Most importantly, ACT NOW! Taking action is always

the hardest step. It's easy to tell yourself that you will tomorrow or when that big, important project your people are engaged in is completed, then...

Remember, if you do not achieve sustainable growth and profitability by disarming the dual threats of ever increasing global competition and industry disruption, all those other projects and plans you worked so hard on aren't going to matter.

Establishing Strategic Innovation as the primary driver of your company and its people is the best assurance you can have that your company will have a future!

"Either we disrupt or we get disrupted!"

- John Chambers, CISCO's visionary CEO, 2015

Do you want and need help? If you do, then turn the page and obtain the help you need.

Just DO IT NOW!

Accelerating the Process – SIC

When I'm hiring someone I look for magic and a spark. Little things that intuitively give me a gut feeling that this person will go to the ends of the earth to accomplish the task at hand."

- Tony Mottle
Former Sony Chairman

Strategic Innovation Consulting

John Di Frances is a highly skilled professional open innovation consultant and strategic planning facilitator, experienced at leading executive teams through the strategic thinking, planning and open innovation process. He understands that the the final outcome will only be as effective as the discussion from which it flows. John engages everyone on the leadership team to fully participate. His goal is to maximize value by focusing the team's attention on high potential opportunities.

As an outsider, he is able both to integrate new ideas, thinking and solutions from other industries into the discussion and ensure that no 'sacred cows' prevent full consideration of all applicable issues. For those organizations that require additional assistance in implementing and monitoring the results of the actionable strategies of their strategic plan, he also offers optional implementation services to assist your team.

How Deep & Wide is Your Knowledge & Experience?

What John, as an expert consultant and facilitator, brings to your leadership team is the extensive outside knowledge and cross industry experience that your organization lacks. Even more critically, he provides an experienced, globally competitive perspective and a unique way of thinking and *'seeing'* which is likely missing from within your organization.

Your organization's vision and frame of reference, literally, your paradigms, define how you perceive every new challenge and opportunity you face. Often, upon meeting a potential new client for the first time, John is asked the question, *"You are not from our industry and don't know our business intimately, so how can you possibly help us?"* His response is, *"That is precisely how I can help you. You and your personnel are experts in your business and industry. Would engaging a consultant with similar knowledge and experience of your business and industry infuse anything new in terms of fresh ideas and perspectives?"*

Put another way, your organization's internal industry knowledge and experience is a mile deep but probably only an inch wide; whereas John's maybe an inch deep in your business, but a mile wide across many industries. What you do know is certainly very important, **but what you don't know is equally important and far more dangerous to your organization's future**. Today, most market disruptions occur suddenly from outside of the industry they disrupt. Focusing exclusively on your industry alone is equivalent to driving your car with all of the windows blacked out, except the windshield.

John has enjoyed the privilege of driving a NASCAR stock car. From the driver's seat, he had a clear view of the racetrack ahead, but was literally blind to everything else. For this reason he, like every NASCAR driver, had a spotter located high above in the grandstand who tells the driver where surrounding cars are positioned and when it is safe to pull out to pass and pull back in again.

When John founded the firm in 1983, 95% of the dangers and threats facing clients originated within their industry – a competitor launching a new product or service, two competitors merging into a formidable powerhouse or a similar occurrence. Today, 90% of the risks facing companies originate from outside of their industry. Think Apple. It transformed the personal computer industry, the mobile computing industry, the telephone industry, the photography industry, the music industry…and more.

What you don't know will hurt you! In fact, if you will review the litany of Fortune companies that have literally vanished from the business landscape over the past decade, you will realize that what you do not know, MAY EVEN KILL YOUR COMPANY! Benchmarking and emulating your competitors or industry leaders can neither lead you to marketplace breakthroughs and dominance nor save your organization, when an outsider suddenly disrupts your industry.

The world is too small, too connected and too globally competitive for you to hide from accelerating change, technology and disruptive competition. There are simply too many companies and bright individuals with voracious marketplace appetites who are developing innovative new products, services, technologies and business models and today, there is no business or industry which is safe!

When John consults on strategy and innovation or facilitates executive teams, he pushes them to think far beyond their experience and comfort zone. He also challenges them at every turn. Do they find this uncomfortable? 'At first,' but once they get into it, they also find it to be an incredibly freeing and rewarding experience. We all live in the glass houses of habit, method, process and system. These are not necessarily 'bad,' but they can become a mental prison, confining our thinking and creating a false sense of security. As a veteran innovation and strategic planning consultant and facilitator, John knows how to redirect conversations from a status quo context to visualizing the 'possible.' He leads and challenges the group in exploring the realm of unlimited possibilities. Accelerated strategic innovation demands a collaborative effort of intense thinking, but it is also incredibly rewarding to move from a 'rut' to the 'possible'.

As an innovation facilitator, John has been assisting organizations globally in their Strategy and Open Innovation activities for thirty years, offering critical insight into the analysis and consequent assessment of key issues as well as assumptions and their resulting limiting constraints. His focus is the development and implementation of high ROI innovation strategies. He has successfully aided corporations, government agencies and nonprofit organizations in board meetings, high dollar value 'must-win' negotiations, senior executive strategic thinking and planning meetings, strategic scenario planning, acquisition and divestiture discussions as well as many other instances. His goal is to rapidly move the organization forward to achieve targeted objectives for sustainable success through disruptive breakthroughs.

Additional Services

Strategic Scenario Planning

Strategic Scenario Planning is a methodology developed by Shell Oil Corporation in the early 1970's, designed to minimize the negative impact of unforeseen future crisis situations through the careful analysis of potential internal and external vulnerabilities followed by the development of responsive pre-planning, integrated into current business strategies. Although one cannot completely eliminate all major risks, it is both possible and prudent to seek to minimize their negative impact as well as optimize resulting marketplace strategies.

This exercise is known as Strategic Scenario Identification and Response Planning. Just as insurance is necessary to mitigate risk of loss, forward thinking organizations prepare ahead to minimize the potential risk of non-insurable calamity.

If a fire destroyed your office or plant tonight, insurance would cover the loss and disruption, but do you have plans in place that would enable your personnel to resume their business functions in an orderly fashion tomorrow morning? Or would your phones simply go silent, leaving your customers wondering what happened to you. Would you have an expedient means of contacting your own employees and keeping them informed? Do you have pre-established plans which can instantly be activated in the event that a major supplier experiences a catastrophic event which severely impacts your business. This can and does happen.

In late 2015, Chipotle restaurants experienced a series of E. coli customer food poisoning events. It was later determined that three different pathogens caused the six known outbreaks across a number of states. The company leadership's slow response in identifying the sources and eliminating the problem suggests that they were unprepared to quickly and effectively address the crisis through preplanning. Finally, four months after the first October 2015 outbreaks, on February 8th, 2016, the company closed all of its stores for a few hours to enable company wide food safety employee training to address the specific causes. This delayed response cost the company dearly in terms of losses in revenue, profits, company image, customer loyalty and market-share as well as the numerous additional customer lawsuits.

The alternative to Strategic Scenario Planning is to do nothing until a natural or man-made disaster strikes and paralyzes your business. Strategic Scenario Planning can be performed either as an integrated part of Strategic Planning or as a stand-alone exercise and is beneficial for any size organization.

The Legacy Project

The Legacy Project directs the organization's leadership's attention to the intangible aspects of organizational growth and success, recognizing that when these values become the primary focus of our goal setting and efforts, the desired tangible outcomes such as profit growth, increased customer satisfaction and retention, increased productivity, loyalty and employee commitment will become natural outcomes. The Legacy Project is premised upon well documented evidence that principled leaders empower their people to collaborate effectively, seize creative opportunities and accomplish synergistic results. This is the secret to unleashing continuous gains in organizational productivity and growth.

For more information, visit:

TheLegacyProject.us

Your next action steps begin on page 67.

SIC

Strategic Innovation Consulting

For more information visit us at:

www.StrategicInnovation.Consulting

or

Contact us at 1.262.922.1101

Helping Senior Executives Achieve
Sustainable Growth and Profitability through
Strategy & Innovation

We Just DO IT!

"Hope is not a Strategy!"

- U.S. Air Force Special Operations Pilot

SIC - StrategicInnovation.Consulting

SIC - StrategicInnovation.Consulting

Next Action Steps

To Do 1st

What:_____

_____

_____

_____

When:_____

_____

By what means:_____

_____

_____

_____

To Do 2nd

What:_____

_____

_____

_____

When:_____

_____

By what means:_____

_____

_____

_____

To Do 3rd

What:_____

_____

_____

_____

When:_____

_____

By what means:_____

_____

_____

_____

Notes:

_____

_____

_____

_____

_____

_____

_____

_____

_____

_____

_____

_____

_____

_____

_____

_____

_____

_____

_____

_____

_____

SIC - StrategicInnovation.Consulting

_____

_____

_____

_____

_____

_____

_____

_____

_____

_____

_____

_____

_____

_____

_____

_____

_____

_____

_____

_____

Just DO IT NOW!

SIC - StrategicInnovation.Consulting

You may choose to delay,
but Time, your Competitors
and the Disruptors will NOT!